Oil Painting

Masterful Techniques to Oil Painting, Portrait Painting and Landscape Painting

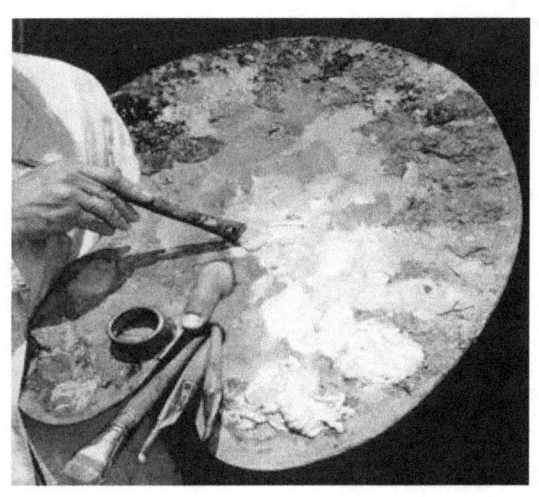

Judith Ann Miller

Judith Ann Miller

contained within this document, including, but not limited to, —
errors, omissions, or inaccuracies.

Table of Contents

Introduction

I want to thank you and congratulate you for purchasing the book, *"Oil Masterful Techniques to Oil Painting, Portrait Painting and Landscape Painting"*.

This book contains proven steps and strategies on how to start your oil painting journey. It contains discussions on painting tools, principles and techniques that every beginner should know before they become masters of oil painting. It also has some exercises broken down in steps for you to practice some of those painting techniques.

The book was written with new oil painters in mind, as it takes a little time to get accustomed to the different techniques involved in oil painting. This book should give you all the information that you need to know to start this hobby and you will also be able to add techniques of your own to the experience, once you have started out using the traditional methods outlined within this book.

Judith Ann Miller

Art is a very individual thing and it's very important to be able to put your individualism onto the canvas, though you do need to know the techniques that help you to do this. As oil paints are permanent, you need to understand how to manipulate your images, how to use a spatula or knife to create texture and how to apply paints in the right way. Once these techniques are learned, they give you a great grounding for actually becoming the individual artist that you are.

Even classic painters have had to learn the techniques before going on to producing wonderful images that we see in galleries every day. Join them and know that the beginning of this journey was also experienced by great painters who left their mark behind them. Your paintings today may be the masterpieces of tomorrow.

Thanks again for purchasing this book, I hope you enjoy it!

Chapter 1 – Tools of the Trade

Like with all other projects, the first step to painting will always be preparation. Of course, an important part of the preparatory phase would be gathering the right tools together. If you have a good local art store, you will probably find what you need to start out will be easily available at prices that are not too expensive. You can, however, check out prices against website prices, since the Internet opens up a whole new market. It is possible to buy good quality products online at cheaper prices but don't forget to check out what the postage costs as this may make a potential bargain less attractive.

Here are some painting tools and supplies that you will be using when you start to use oils as a medium for painting:

Oil Paint

You can find a large variety of oil paints available in various places. Your best bet is at a local art store, but you can also try ordering them online. The paints would vary in terms of price, quality and even safety of use.

Your basic oil paint has two components: the pigment and the oil. The pigment is what gives it color. It used to be made of substances that are found in nature like minerals or even plants. You can still find these types of paint for sale, but most pigment is now synthetic and made to be cheaper and more resistant to fading. The oil is what gives the paint its name apparently. It is what binds the pigments together. This can come in a wide variety depending on what is available to you. Take note that some pigments can be toxic. Make sure to check the labels carefully before you buy your paint and if you buy paints that you are unsure of, keep them safely away from children.

Here are some important things you should check for as well:

- Water-Soluble and Traditional

  The main difference between the two is the manner of thinning the paint. Traditional oil paints usually require some substance like turpentine to act as a thinner and also to clean brushes. These can have very strong odors and can even be hazardous. Water-soluble paints, as the name suggests, dissolve in water. They are the same as traditional paints except that the oils are modified to allow mixing or dissolving in water making them easier to clean off or thin. Water-soluble paints usually perform the same as traditional paint but some are still of the opinion that traditional paint is best. If you are still learning and starting out, water-soluble is probably the way to go to start your experience.

- Grade

You can find paint in basically two grades: student and professional. You will find that student grade paint is cheaper but it contains less pigment than that of professional paint. If you are not too keen on spending too much while studying painting, student grade is a fine choice. But if you do not mind the bump in price, professional grade paint is the choice for better quality and for giving wonderful color.

- Lightfastness

This simply refers to the resistance of the paint to fading. Some paints are prone to fading. This is especially true when left in direct sunlight. Most manufacturers will label their paints. If not, you can always consult the seller who should have the information on their products. If you notice in galleries, people are asked not to photograph old oil paintings. This is because of the lightfastness and the old masters were usually painted with paints which do not have the modern qualities of lightfastness.

Mediums, Solvents and Thinners

Mediums refer to substances that are mixed with paint to alter it in some way. Some mediums can change the drying time of the paint, slowing it down or speeding it up depending on your needs. If you have a studio with not much space and want work to dry quickly, these are useful. Some may also make the paint flow more, change the consistency, the transparency and even the glossiness. The use of mediums would depend on your style and your desired effect. The next chapter will discuss a way in which mediums can be used for certain painting techniques. Though you can usually buy the mediums you need, they can also be mixed and custom made to the preference of the artist.

You can also find substances called thinners and solvents. These are used for dissolving or thinning the paints to make them easier to work with, create a certain consistency of paint, make modifications or corrections to your painting, or for cleaning your paint brushes and materials. As earlier mentioned, these are primarily for traditional paints. Water-soluble paints only require water to do the job.

Brushes

Painting brushes come in several kinds. It is a good idea to keep with you a good variety of brushes as they all have their own uses. Here are some things to look out for when selecting your brushes:

- Size

  You will usually start a painting off using bigger brushes for the rough sectioning of your painting and the like. Then as you go more into the detail in your work, you will likely use progressively smaller brushes. Thus, having a variety is essential.

- Shape

  The tips of the brush come in several shapes that affect how the paint is transferred onto the surface. You have the usual types: Rounds, Flats Filberts, and Riggers.

  - Rounds – round body that ends in a point. Usually used for details.

- Flats – wide, flat hairs that end in a squared tip. Large ones like those used in painting houses are for painting large portions of the surface. Smaller ones can be used to put in straight or chiseled details.

- Filberts – almost the same as flats but have rounded ends or even pointed ones for adding detail in a particular way.

- Riggers – round body but slender and longer hairs compared to rounds. Used for making longer brushstrokes. These are used a lot in easel work and it's a good idea to get used to using one as this is also used to hold up to measure for scale while you work.

- Brush Length

This refers to the length of the handle. Longer handles allow you to make broader strokes while shorter handles are good for making small and detailed touches. This is however dependent on your preference, style, and the way in which you will use it. Portrait artists tend to use longer handles because they want to stand back from the work and see the detail from a distance. Close up, this is very hard to do.

- Type of Hair

Brushes usually have either fine or coarse hair. Of course, you can find some that are degrees in between. The important thing to consider is that coarser brushes are usually easier to clean and possibly more durable. They can also hold more thick paint. Soft hair brushes on the other hand are usually used for fine detail work and create smoother strokes. Whatever you buy, do not opt for cheap brushes. The type of hair should be natural rather than synthetic.

- Length of Hair

Shorter hair brushes hold less paint than longer hair ones. Also short hair brushes tend to be stiff compared to long hair ones. You will need both types so don't be lulled into a false sense of security thinking that one brush will cover all events. As you begin to work with oils, you will find that the more choices you have, the better the work you can produce. There are always awkward moments when you wish you had another shape of brush or a different length of bristle, so buy a variety.

Judith Ann Miller

Palettes

These are the tools for holding your paint. Incidentally, you can also mix paint on them before and as you paint. You can find them in several shapes and sizes. What you should consider is finding one that has enough room for your paint and mixing but is not too much of a hassle to handle. Make sure that you can carry it around comfortably if you plan to. Some have a finger hole but rather than buying a small one with a finger hole, bear in mind that small sizes may restrict the amount of colors you can work at one time. A larger palette means that you have more flexibility.

A good thing to remember is that you have to clean your palette before you start painting. Any oil paint that dries on it cannot be reused. Incidentally, you can also find disposable palettes in the form of palette pads. You just tear the used piece after each session and you have a brand new one again. Remember when you are mixing paints that you may want to produce the same color again. It may sound wasteful, but you can mix a larger amount to be sure you have enough, and this is wiser than actually mixing smaller amounts unless you can keep a note of the ingredients and duplicate your mix. You can with experience, but it takes a while to get that familiar with the use of the paints.

Painting Surfaces

Painting surfaces are where you do your magic with your paint. You have a multitude of choices when it comes to where you want to paint. This depends mostly on what you want to achieve. Remember that choosing the painting surface is as important as choosing the paint to use in terms of the quality and characteristics of your finished painting. Take note of the texture, size and ease of storage. Here are some of the common choices:

- Stretched Canvas

  This is probably the most common option. It is canvas that is pulled over a frame or bars usually made of wood. What you should look for are frames that are strong enough to handle the size of canvas. You can also find canvas made out of either cotton or linen. Cotton is usually the cheaper of the two. The downside is that it loosens more over time than linen. You should likewise pay attention to the texture of the material. You want a fine material if you plan on making detailed paintings. If you plan on using thick layers of paint, the coarser material may be ideal. You may also want to incorporate the texture into the painting itself.

- Plywood or Masonite Panels

You can find these panels in your local art stores already prepared for you to paint on. They are cheaper and can also be homemade. There is also a variety that has canvas glued on to it. This gives you the texture of canvas while also providing a backing which is more rigid than stretched canvas. This is ideal for wall panels.

- Cradled Plywood or Masonite Panels

Some panels also come with frames much like stretched canvas. They are meant to prevent the wood from warping and make them stronger as the panels alone may be easy to bend or break. These would be good for exhibition work.

- Wrapped Panels

Canvas-wrapped panels are made of Masonite, plywood or cardboard, and are wrapped with a primed canvas. They are similar to panels with canvas glued to one side. However, if the core is made of cardboard, the panel may swell and warp over time. These may be an option at the beginning of your work but think about the finished product if you intend to make it a lasting one.

- Canvas Pads

These are basically sheets of canvas that are made into a pad. It is ideal for practicing. You can cut sheets out and attach them to a panel or frame with clamps or glue. Just like stretched canvas, they come in a variety of textures and material.

Easels

Artists traditionally stand while painting. This allows them to move freely and get a better view of their subject and their painting. For this, they usually use easels. Nowadays, easels come in different shapes and sizes depending on what you need as long as they hold your paintings in position.

When choosing an easel, consider if it is appropriate for the size of your intended painting and your workplace. You can find some that are designed for standing or sitting. You can also find some that are designed for tables. There are also those meant for indoor and outdoor painting. Make sure that you find one that you will be comfortable using for long periods of time. A handy tip is to look for easels that are adjustable, portable and easy to move or store. The more adjustment you have, the better, as you can change the height of the picture to suit the stance you will be using when painting.

A good quality easel may set you back a bit, but it's worth it long term and if you don't get on with oil painting, you can sell these on, as artists are always looking for good quality easels.

Other Tools

There are other tools that you can look into when you buy your supplies. Survey your local art store and see if they have the following. You may not use all of them now and may not even need them altogether. Nonetheless they can be helpful depending on your project and what you want to do:

- Rags/Towels – for wiping and cleaning

- Palette Knife – for handling your paint, mixing, and even painting

- Fixative Spray – prevents smudging of graphite or coal sketches

- Kneaded Eraser – a special type of eraser that does not crumble

Things to Avoid

When looking for supplies for the first time, you might not be sure what to look for and might end up buying everything in sight. While it is not really a problem if you can afford to buy all your supplies at once, it is good to know what things to avoid when you are starting out.

- Unusually Cheap Paint – these usually are of inferior or dubious quality. Stick to student grade paint that your art store recommends. Do not buy unlabeled paint no matter how cheap it is. The problem with cheap paints is that the pigments are likely to be weak and the paints may even be more toxic with little indication of the dangers shown on the labels.

- Toxic Pigments – read the labels of paint tubes. Some pigments are harmful when not handled properly. If the paint tube does not have warnings or you are unsure, ask the art store. You can try these out if you want when you have more experience with painting. The toxicity levels are something you can get accustomed to and the reason that toxic paints are chosen is because the pigments are much stronger in color. However, they are not the best for a beginner.

- Very Big or Small Paint Tubes – when you buy large tubes of paint, chances are you will keep them around for a long time. The stress of reusing a tube such as opening it over and over can cause the tube to deteriorate and eventually split. As for small tubes, you will find that they will not last long enough to finish a painting. This is a hassle and a waste of money as it is usually more expensive to buy two small tubes than a regular sized one. Stick with a regular sized tube of paint. This will also get you accustomed to handling your paints and learning to close them off properly to preserve the liquidity of the paints.

Chapter 2 – Basic Principles

Doing great work with painting is all about three things: Structure, Color and Value. Before you jump into creating your masterpiece, here are the basics.

How to Draw Structures

You may already have experience in drawing before you decided to start painting. If not, you have nothing to worry about as it is not really as complicated as it looks. When you start drawing before you paint, you have to keep in mind that you are trying to simplify what you are observing. This is what is called structural drawing. This is the foundation of most artwork and it is a fine thing to learn.

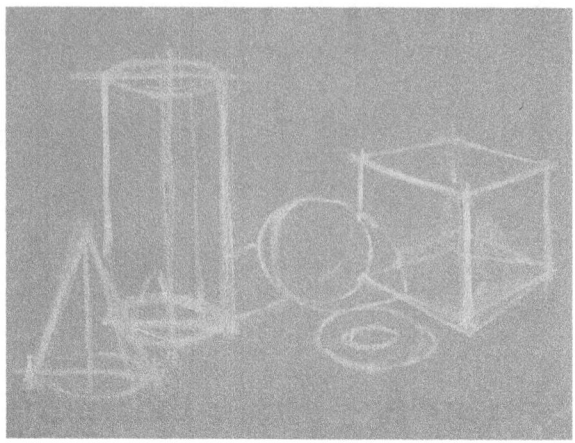

The image is only accurate in that it gives you a structural outline of what the eye sees. It does not have to be accurate in detail, more in sizes and shapes.

Here is a quick rundown of how to do structural drawings:

Imagine what you want to paint as just simple shapes put together. This means circles, squares, triangles and the like. Visualize this as you look at your subject.

1. Visualize Big Shapes

    Draw the obvious shapes that you see. The biggest ones are where you should start. The reason you are doing this is to give your painting some kind of perspective and shape.

2. Fit in the Smaller Shapes

As you go, look for the smaller shapes that make up your subject and draw them in. The human face, for example, may consist of many shapes and you can help yourself to get accurate detail by using these shapes for your initial sketch.

3. Fill in the Details

Now that you have the general shapes in, start putting details to your drawing to make it as accurate as you want it to be. Remember art is about your interpretation.

Measurement and Proportion

Another important aspect of structure is proportion. This is what makes your art look right. Whether you want your art to be accurate or just believable, this is the way to go. Using correct proportions makes your art believable.

To get the proper proportion you need to make measurements. You can usually do this with a ruler, a pencil or even your brush. If you are working with a subject that you can easily measure, like a small object or even a photograph, a ruler can do an excellent job.

The problem would usually arise when you have to measure from a distance. This is how you do it:

1. Keep your arm straight when you do this. Hold it out in front of you while holding your measuring tool. Some artists use a long paintbrush for this purpose. Use your thumb and the tip of the tool as the start and end point of your measurement.

2. Position the top of the tool so that it is also at the top of the subject as you see it. Use your thumb to mark the end of your measurement.

3. While keeping your thumb where you made your measurement, reposition your tool to compare with the other dimensions of your subject.

Other ways of measuring

In this day and age, it's a good idea to use an iPad to help you to get the right measurements. There are some great apps which will help you. By taking a photograph of the image, some of these programs are able to produce a grid over the top of the image and this helps you to create the same proportions on the canvas because you can also pencil a grid on the canvas and make sure that the details appear in the correct squares. This system is very good for getting all the measurements correct and is used for very detailed work such as portraits. Used on the National Portraiture Competition in the United Kingdom, this proved to be a very popular way to get the measurement of details correct. It's also great for placing eyes and facial features in exactly the right place.

Perspective

You can make your work look like it shows distance and depth through perspective. This is another aspect of structure. You can choose to use linear perspective or two-point perspective to make your work pop out like a three-dimensional image.

The three things you have to keep in mind when making your first drawings is where you place the horizon, where the vanishing point is and the vantage point you want to use. This is a challenging subject for beginners to drawing but once you get the hang of it, it will be a breeze.

Perspective is also gained by using shadow in your painting. This helps to give items in the picture shape and form so that they are not seen as flat. If you look at great masters, they know how to use shading to create this depth and it's a good idea to study the masters and see the different methods that they used.

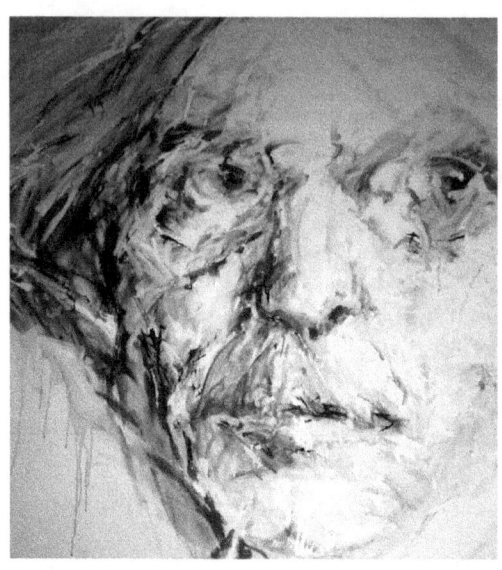

Look how the shadow in this painting is being used to build up the character of the face. It's clever use of shading. This is built up bit by bit during the course of the painting as more detail is added. What this is beginning to create is a realistic image of the face which has the size and measurement correct. What needs to be done after this stage is building up the layers of paint to create the perfect representation of the face being painted.

Colors

The best way to understand colors is to use a color wheel. You can usually find printed versions of color wheels at your local art store which comes with tips and tricks. You can also simply find one online for free. If you want to practice some painting, you can even make your own using the paint you have so you can get a feel of how to mix colors. Here are some important points to remember about colors:

- Primary Colors

  These are the most basic of them. They include blue, red and yellow. All other colors are made from a combination of these three. Remember this when mixing.

- Secondary Colors

  These are combinations of two primary colors. They are green, purple and orange.

- Tertiary Colors

  These are colors that result from combining a primary color with the secondary color next to it.

- Complementary Colors

  These refer to the colors that are at opposite sides of each other on a color wheel. Take note that any pair of complimentary colors are made up of the three primary colors. If you mix both complimentary colors together you will come up with a neutral grayish brown. Also, if you want to mute a certain color in your work, you can just add its complimentary color.

- Analogous colors

  These refer to a group of colors that are close together on the color wheel. If you take a quarter of the wheel, the colors there would be analogous to each other. If you use these colors together in a painting, it will produce a pure and bright effect.

Values

A value in painting refers to the how light or dark a color is. This goes into the use of shading, how you portray shadows and the contrast of the colors you use. Value gives form and depth to your painting. Here are important things to take note of:

- Contrast

  The difference in values is called the contrast. Greater difference means more contrast. If you use values that are similar, you create a low contrast painting. It is tame and muted. Using varying values makes a high contrast painting. It has more depth. Many modern artists prefer to have a lot of contrast while more traditional artists may be more subtle in their approach.

- Source of Light

When you paint, know where the light is coming from and what kind of light is it. This greatly affects how you paint your scene and how you assign values. The direction, brightness, even color of the light can have varying effects on what you paint.

This causes particular difficulty for people who are painting scenery, since the colors change so much with the changing light. A good oil painter will take photographs when the light is perfect so that they can continue to work on the image once the painting is taken back to the studio. These photographs are valuable resources and it's worthwhile investing in a good digital camera so that you can see the light very clearly in the image that you have on the camera at the same time as working on your canvas.

- Aerial Perspective

A good trick is to consider aerial perspective. This refers to making things look far or near by using values. The farther an object, the more muted it appears to the eye. Notice how faraway things tend to look grayish blue and fuzzy. You can also make distant things look like they are fading away. When you look at the scenery from your window, you will notice that trees which are distant won't be something that will really show clear branches and leaves, whereas those near to you will.

Note what trees look like in reality, rather than trying to paint a tree as you see it in your mind's eye. It may not look anything like a tree in reality but is a mere dot or series of dots in the distance.

The image shown on the next page gives you a perfect example of when a tree or a bush doesn't look like a bush but is represented by shapes. That's an important lesson to learn. You need to paint what you see as opposed to what you think your picture should show.

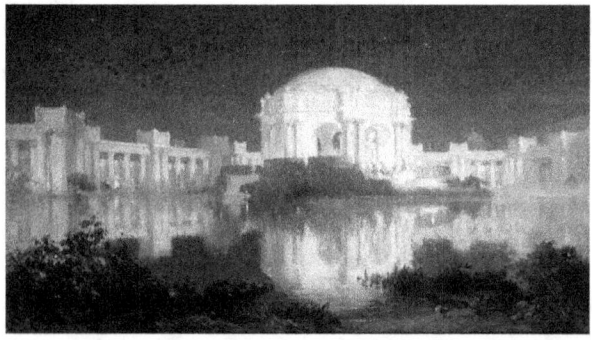

In this Palace of Fine Arts image, look how important structure is to the finished product but notice that the trees and bushes in the picture are merely series of paint strokes rather than being detailed imagery. In the distance, against the building, there are bushes but these are mere dots with a little shading, rather than being fully drawn shrubs. You need to gain perspective of how the smaller items fit into the picture, rather than trying to give detail that a viewer would not actually see if looking from the perspective shown in the image.

It's always good practice to try several brushes and several techniques for getting those small details the way that you want them to be. If you need to work on a smaller canvas to try out different paintbrushes, you may find this to be very helpful indeed.

Judith Ann Miller

Chapter 3 – Basic Techniques

When you are familiar with the tools and the principles of oil painting, it is time to put them together. It is wise to learn a few techniques and practice them before you start painting your first project. This way, you will be more confident and comfortable when you finally begin. There's a lot that goes into an oil painting and mixing your actual paints will happen once you are happy with your sketches and have the basic shapes in place. Don't be too quick to mix colors. Be happy with the proportion of your sketch because it's easy to correct a sketch, while repainting an area can be painstakingly difficult.

Mixing Your Paint

One of the fun things about oil painting is mixing colors of paint. For optimal results, you should consider using the right colors and make sure you use enough of the paint. You want to ensure that you mix the paint in a thorough manner. Most of the time you will be doing this on your palette but you may also find that mixing as you paint on the surface can have interesting results. Here are some suggestions for you when mixing:

- When mixing paint, you should lead with the light colors. Then you add in the darker colors. Remember that light colors are less dominant than the dark ones. Since you will be generally using more light than dark, it is good to add only small bits of dark colors to your palette whereas you add bigger amounts of light colors. This is to conserve paint because oil paints do not stay fresh too long once they are on your palette.

- You should try to remember how valuable gray is as a color. Gray will help you to calm down a color which is too bright and is achieved of course by mixing black and white. If you can buy a gray color, then it's always a valuable one to have in your paint box because you can use it to tone down colors that haven't quite worked out as muted as you wish. Gray mutes colors and gives them a very fine quality that can't be achieved in the same way with bright colors.

- You should also consider using a palette knife when mixing your paint. While you might find it easy to mix paint with your brush, the palette knife is better at scooping that paint up. Trying to scoop paint with a brush might lead to clogging or damage. It's also so much easier to clean a palette knife than to clean a brush. When you are mixing paint, much of the paint will get into the stock of the brush and that's particularly hard to remove. You can also damage your brushes very easily by using them for the mixing process, whereas you can wipe your palette knife clean between mixes.

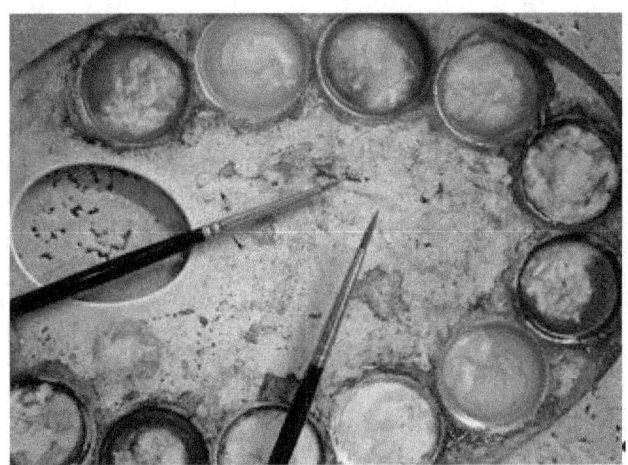

Loading Your Brush

When you load your brush with paint, keep in mind how you intend to use the paint. The amount you use will usually affect how it will look on the surface. Here are tips on how to load your brush; of course you can find other ways that will suit your style:

How much paint do you want on your brush? The amount of paint you load on a brush depends on how you plan to apply the paint. Push loading and pull loading are two ways to load a brush. Use the push loading method if you want to grab a lot of paint onto your brush for applying a thick layer of paint. Use the pull loading method to load a smaller amount of paint onto your brush.

- You use the push loading method if you want to use thick layers of paint. You do this by pushing into the paint with your brush. This can be tough on your paint brush and is best done with filbert or flat brushes.

- You use the pull loading method when you want to use less paint. You do this by dragging your brush onto the paint. The amount of paint is determined by the angle of your brush as you pull.

- Take care not to overload your brush. This makes it hard to control and might lead to damage. Always wipe or clean your brush if you happen to choke it with paint.

Some Brushstrokes

If you try to experiment with your brush, you will find that it can actually produce several strokes depending on how you use it. The angle and how you grip it for example, can lead to different looking results with the use of a flat brush.

Here are some common brushstrokes that you can use and alter when painting:

- A Wide Stroke Using a Filbert or Flat

  Use the edge of the brush that is perpendicular to the stroke. You want to use the width of your brush bristles.

- A Thin Stroke Using a Filbert or Flat

  Hold the brush perpendicular to the surface. It should only be the edge of the bristles that is touching the surface. Then pull the brush to the side to make a line.

- Dabbing Paint Using a Filbert or Flat

  You use this to put paint onto a wet surface. Position the brush almost flat on the surface. Then dab paint on using the flat part of the bristles.

- A Wide Stroke Using a Round

Lay the brush slightly flat to the surface. Use the body of the round bristles instead of the tip.

- A Thin Stroke Using a Rigger or Round

Using smaller brushes can make thinner strokes easy. You can also use bigger round brushes by using only the tip and keeping the brush upright.

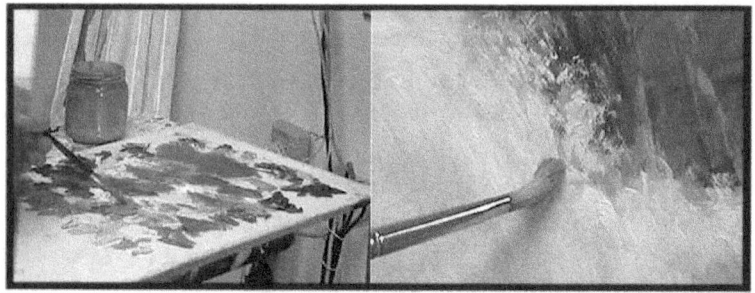

Some Techniques in Painting

Here are a few techniques you can try out and combine as you work. Experiment and modify them to your liking:

- Glazing

This means putting thin, wet paint onto dry paint. This helps you achieve finer details.

- Wash

This is a transparent paint application. It has been diluted with water or thinner. Use it to lay a ground where you can paint on or on its own.

- Impasto

This is simply a thick application of paint. It can use much more paint than other techniques.

- Scumbling

This is a technique of applying undiluted paint onto dried paint. The effect is achieved when some of the dry paint's texture and color shows through.

- Alla Prima

This is a technique that involves quickly painting to achieve the general appearance of your finished work. This means putting down the structure and colors to look close to how it will look when you are done. After that, you simply add the details to finish the work.

Using Under-paintings or Under-drawings

This simply means planning your painting by either drawing on the surface or painting on it beforehand. Use a pencil, charcoal or paint to define the basic structures of your work so you can just fill it in with details when you paint. You can define light and dark areas of your work before you apply color to it. When using pencil or charcoal, it is useful to use fixing sprays to avoid smearing. For paint, it is usually good to use thin applications. You can use this to lay down the dark areas with paint as if it were a ground.

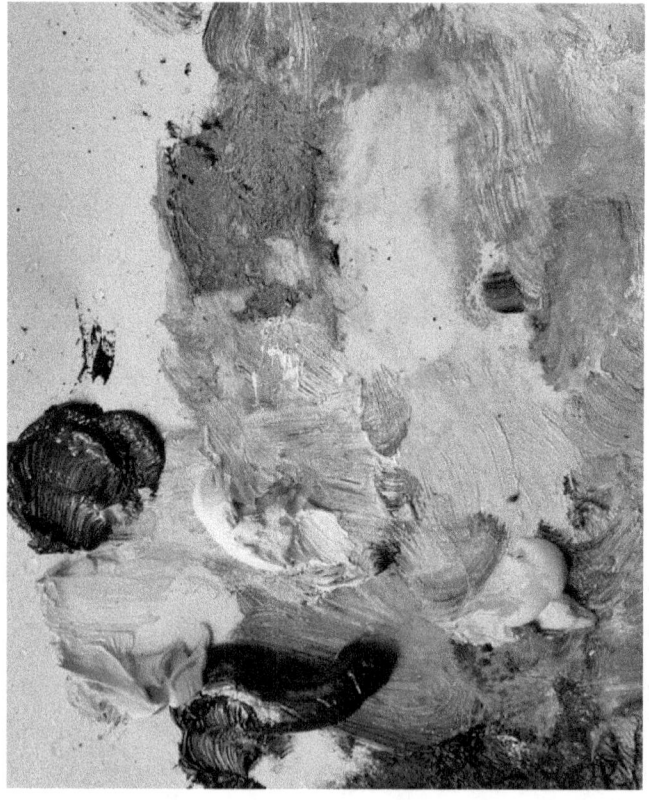

The palette shown above shows what your palette will look like when you are in the process of mixing paints. Notice the larger blobs of paint. These are paints which are still moist enough to be used, whereas the flat paints are likely to be dryer. If you want to keep your paints moist while you work, try to work in a very organized manner so that your moist paints are in sufficient quantity to stay moist. Air dries oil paints quite rapidly when laid flat on the palette.

It's worthwhile scraping your palette occasionally when the paint is getting low because the palette knife can help you to keep the palette workable, and will help you to keep your palette fairly clean. Build-up of paint will make the palette surface uneven and that's difficult to work with when you are trying to create uniform color mixes.

Judith Ann Miller

Chapter 4 – Study 1: The World in Monochrome

Monochromatic painting is a good way to practice how to apply values to your painting. You can look for photographs that are in monochrome and show simple shapes. What you want to do is practice how direction of light affects your subject and how shadows and highlights can be made to look realistic by playing with simple contrast.

Here is a simple step-by-step on how to do a monochromatic painting:

You will need:

- Sample Photo of Simple Objects (like rocks, or balls in monochrome)
- Small Painting Surface (of your choice)
- Gray and White Paint (preferably Payne's Gray and Titanium White)

- Filberts (number 2 and 8)
- Rigger (number 4)
- Pencil/Charcoal (with fixative spray and eraser)
- Palette
- Rags
- Easel
- Water
- Palette Knife
- Others like thinner or medium

Things to remember:

- Values
- Light Source
- Under-drawing/Under-painting

First, identify where the light is coming from to guide you on how to apply shadow and highlight. Take not of the lightest and darkest areas of the photograph. Visualize the simple shapes that you will use.

1. Use a rag to apply a ground. Use diluted gray paint to make a transparent layer of paint on the surface. Do not worry about how neat or complete it is since you will paint over it anyway.

2. Make an under-drawing of your shapes when the ground is dry. You can also use paint instead to make an under-painting even while the ground is wet. Start from the

central object and work your way outwards to keep things in position.

3. Start painting the objects in using mixtures of white and gray. Take note again of which areas should be dark and light. Adjust your mixtures to address this. Use the bigger filbert to fill in the shapes. Lighten and darken the objects to improve it.

4. Start blending your light and dark paint to match those of the subject. Use the bigger and smaller filbert to fill in the objects as necessary.

5. Blend the colors and define the dark areas in between each of them.

6. Use the number 2 filbert to adjust the dark areas and make the objects more defined.

7. Now add the highlights using the number 2 filbert and white paint. You can also use the rigger to add more fine details.

8. When you are satisfied, sign in your name. You are done!

Remember that you can work your picture in areas where you are unhappy with the finish and it helps you to be able to work out which brushes create which effects. Practice using your brushes because you will find that you will have favorites for different aspects of a picture. Some artists like fine brushes for detail, whereas others prefer to use brushes which are wider but use them so that only the end of the bristles touches the canvas.

Chapter 5 – Study 2: Trees!

Most artist paint trees directly without sketching them out first. But painting trees in detail is actually a good way of practicing how under-painting works and a way to practice painting techniques that involve painting over layers. It is also good training on how to mix colors. Plus trees are just fun and natural shapes to paint.

Here is a step-by-step on how to paint trees the detailed way:

You will need:

- Small Painting Surface (of your choice)
- Gray and White Paint (preferably Payne's Gray and Titanium White)
- Cadmium Yellow Light
- Cadmium Orange Hue
- Burnt Sienna

- Sap Green
- Phthalo Blue (Red Shade)
- Round (number 2)
- Filberts (number 2 and 4)
- Pencil/Charcoal (with fixative spray and eraser)
- Palette
- Easel
- Water
- Palette Knife

Things to Remember:

- Structural Drawing
- Analogous Colors
- Glazing
- Scumbling

First identify what kind of tree you want to paint. You can use a sample photograph, use an actual tree or even paint one from imagination.

1. Draw the tree starting with the trunk and the branches. Make an outline of how you want the leaves to be shaped around the tree. When you are done, use the fixative.
2. Now paint the leaves first. Use a mix of Cadmium Yellow and Sap Green. Do this with a filbert (number 4). Do not paint over the branches or the trunk.

3. Use the Cadmium Orange and Burnt Sienna to paint over the branches and trunk. Use the round (number 2) and filbert (number 2). You can add or modify the branches as you paint. Remember that branches should taper off towards their tips.

4. At this point none of the branches should be covered. So it is time to cover some of them with leaves. Add more leaves using a Sap Green and Cadmium Yellow in the mix. Use the filbert (number 2). You can also use leaves to cover some parts of the branches that do not look right.

5. Now just like the monochrome painting, you need to define the light and dark areas. Use the Cadmium Yellow mixed in with green to make light areas. Use the Phtalo Blue mixed with the green or brown to make the darker areas in the leaves or the trunk. Use the filbert (number 2) for this.

6. When you are satisfied, sign your work. Another painting finished!

The backgrounds are something that you can work on as well and if you want a really detailed tree, perhaps your background colors should be more muted and put onto the canvas using the palette knife. Then you can start to detail your tree and really get it to work well with the background.

Another method of painting trees is to use the same system as above to create branches and trunk, but when it comes to putting the foliage onto the trees, try a stiff brush and a dabbing method with your leaf colors. If you have a mixture of the colors you have chosen for the foliage on your palette, you can randomly dab your brush so it picks up more than one color and your leaves will look a lot more realistic. You can then touch up areas of branches between the leaves so that they look natural.

Chapter 6 – Learning to Use Sketching to Enhance Your Paintings

The more you practice your sketching, the more accurate your pictures will get. Sketching before using your oil paints really pulls everything into perspective and shows you exactly where everything on the image should be placed.

Making a portrait from a photograph

If you are working on portraiture, your model will certainly feel happier if your image looks like them. The use of a photograph is very useful because even if your model is not present, you will be able to continue to draw the face ready for painting and will have an idea of the textures and the color palette that makes up the skin tones.

If you have taken a photograph or have one that is fairly good quality, draw a grid over it or use your iPad app to draw a grid over the top of the image. Then draw the grid onto your canvas. It won't matter that you are drawing underneath what will be your oil picture because this drawing helps you to get things accurately drawn. Look at each square of the grid, because what it contains needs to be transferred onto the canvas. Fill out the sketch of each square of your grid with pencil detail so that you can see clearly where each element of the image should be placed. If you get it wrong at this stage, it's not too drastic as you can make adjustments.

When you are happy that the sketch is accurate, you can start to add color to your image and work your oils into the areas of the image so that they correspond with the colors that are shown in your photograph. Take time over details such as eyes, nose, lips etc. because often you need to apply the oil paints with a palette knife to get realistic rendition of what you are seeing.

Practice your sketches of facial features and you will find that it gets to be second nature. Remember that there are no standard ways to sketch facial features because everyone that you draw will be different. Move on to using charcoal as your base medium as this is what was used by the famous artists of the past.

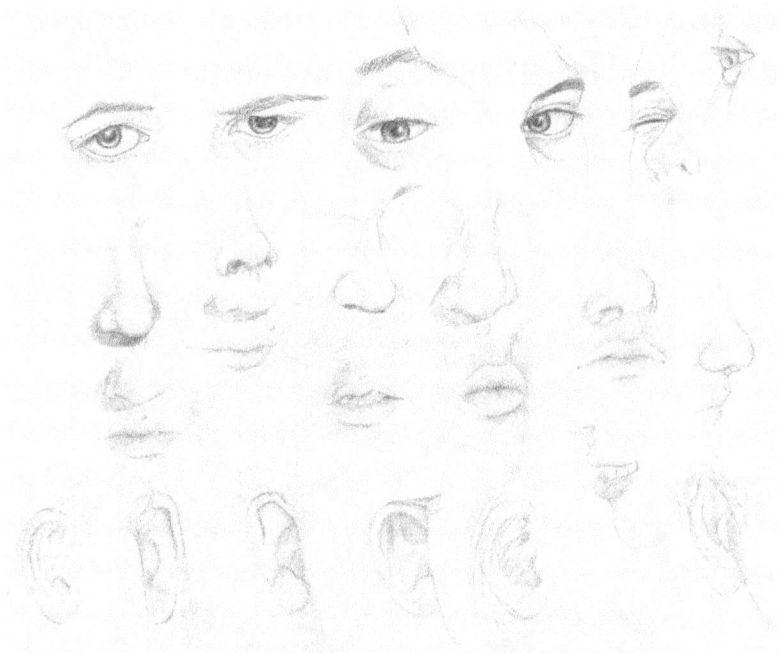

It's not the easiest of things to sketch, but the more accurate you are with your sketching, the easier it is to apply your oil paint and get all the detail right.

The more you sketch and copy photographs, the more you will get accustomed to the different shading which is applied to different areas of the face to help you to create a realistic image.

Look at the amount of detail in this eye. It will help you to see that the pupil and iris are made up of many colors and that it is a combination of these colors that helps you to create a realistic image of an eye. Eyes are difficult because of the glass like rendition needed to make the eye look realistic.

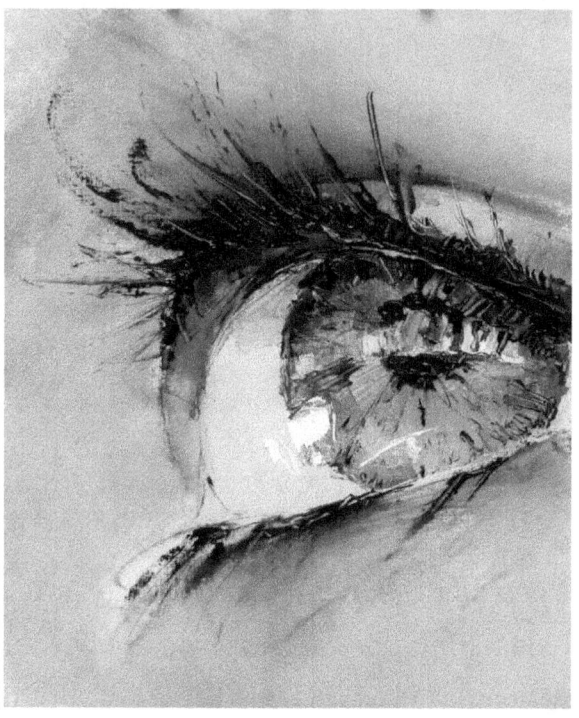

The detail in this picture is amazing and you can produce the same thing by getting used to using your oil paints and your different brush techniques to produce that amount of detail. The reflection created by the use of colors is very clever indeed and makes your image look more realistic. In fact if you look at the eye lashes, these seem to have been put in place with razor precision, and this may have been because of the use of a palette knife. This instrument is first class for producing sharp lines as well as for filling larger areas with smooth color.

Judith Ann Miller

Chapter 7 – Learning all about Skin Tones

When you use oil paints, you may find that you want to experiment with skin tones. Those who are new to painting often try to make the face all one color. Of course, the sketch that you do will guide you and help you to decide where shading needs to be applied, but how do you mix skin tones and blend them together?

If you look at the skin tone color wheel below, which was produced by Neil Harbisson, it shows the tones in general and is a very good guide to mixing colors to create the perfect tones, including shaded areas.

THE HUMAN COLOUR WHEEL
Colour wheel based on the hue and light detected on human skins.

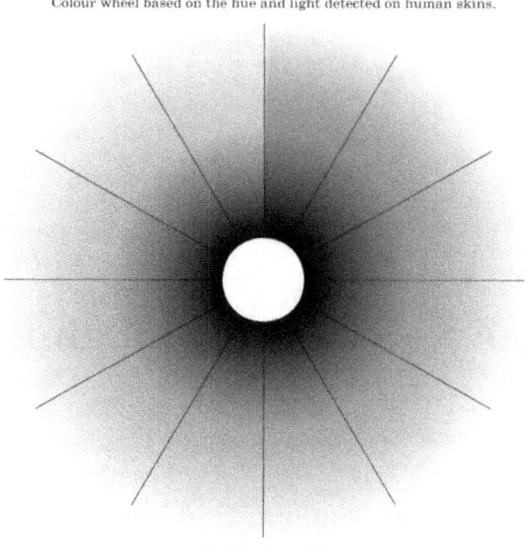

(Neil Harbisson 2009)

Look at the colors to the left hand side of the wheel and these are realistic colors that can be used for the skin, working from the outside of the wheel toward the inside for the actual shading of the skin tone that you have produced. It's a very useful guide to help you to get it right. You may find this hard to believe but to mix the perfect skin tone, you may have to add a color that you may not have thought useful, and that is ultramarine blue. The orange color that you create by mixing yellow ochre, raw umber and red looks too flat to be a real color. The brightness makes the skin look too made up. If you add a little touch of ultramarine blue, what this does is mute the color down to a perfect skin tone. Different amounts of the original colors will produce different shades and you can do a shade test by doing a close-up image of the skin and then color matching while you mix the colors.

You will need darker and lighter versions of the same color for your shading and highlighting and this can be achieved by adding white for paler color or a little more blue to make the shade darker. Those who are expert at painting skin tones use different colors to help give the face character and shading.

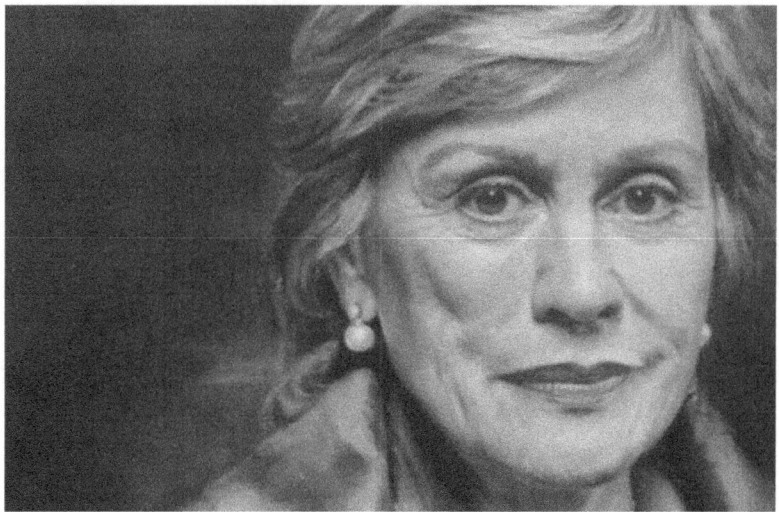

This painting was done by an artist who took part in the Portrait Artist of the Year, but look at the skin tones. They perfectly depict the character and are used very well indeed. Remember that skin tones will be different for different ethnicities and for different ages as the skin gets more pallid with age. Remember, the overall tone of the face is found at the very edge of the skin tone color wheel.

Chapter 8 – Abstract Oil Painting

Many artists enjoy abstract work and use colors that amaze the viewer, as they may not be colors associated with part of what the image represents. The trouble is that people have set ideas about how something should look. If you look into the history of abstract painting, you will find that some works clearly show that it's the artist's representation of the overall image that counts, rather than how accurately the image is caught. Abstract painting means that it is an interpretation rather than being an exact replica of what the artist sees.

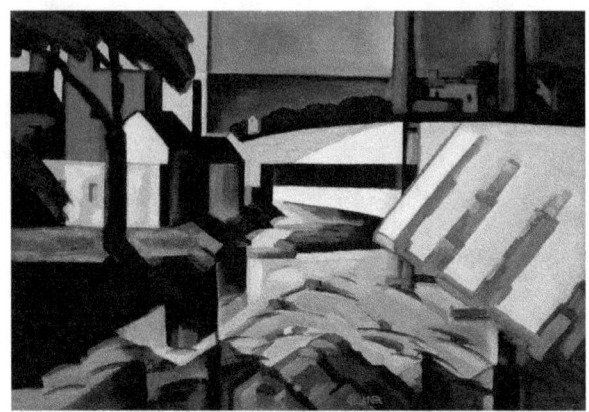

In this painting, the viewer is left to interpret what they see. For example, no one expects a black tree or a purple field in the background, but actually these colors can exist and sometimes do depending upon the light. This artist has produced a scenery picture in oils that looks stunning but has not used the colors and textures that traditional art may have used. Instead, it goes abstract and the artist is given more freedom of expression.

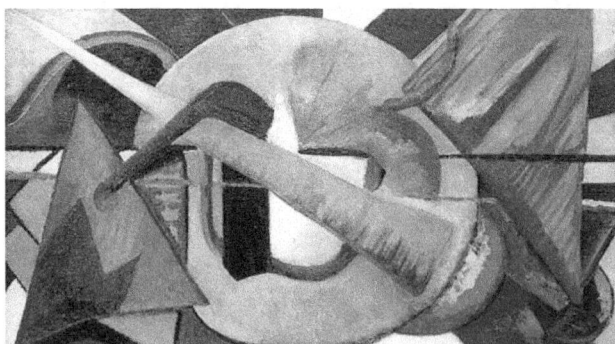

This is another oil painting done in the abstract art style which can be interpreted in many different ways by the viewer. The artist may not have intended it to be interpreted in that way, but that's the beauty of abstract work. It is open to interpretation not only by the artist but by the viewer. The image was produced by Katherine Drieir in 1918 and still looks very modernistic. Looking at the central round shape within the image, one is almost put in mind of an apple, since the shading gives the shape of the apple some substance.

When you create work which is abstract, you are permitted to use artistic license both with color, shape and form, though one can clearly see from the image shown above that some of the principles of classic art still apply to the application of paint onto canvas even if the image is considered as abstract. Look at the lines on the image and the shading is typical of classical representation. It gives the effect of three dimensional imagery. So, even if you want to try abstract painting, don't make the mistake of believe that abstract means slapdash. It is well composed, gives the viewer a really good image to look at and dissect but also employs traditional techniques.

Judith Ann Miller

Chapter 9 – Introducing Wax into Oil Painting

If you are trying out new things, why not try melting some beeswax and mixing it with the pigments or with the paints to see what effect they have? You have to remember that proportions are important. Too much wax and it will eventually come away from the canvas. Too much oil and the wax lose its translucent quality. Get it right, and it's a wonderful medium for raising areas of the oil painting to give the image more texture. There are artists who have been using this method for some time, and the results are astounding. The wax itself gives a new quality to the oil paints and it works wonders on giving the image extra texture.

The other ingredient that is important in the mix is a medium to help the drying process. If you are going to use oil paints instead of just pigments, be aware that the tubes of paint may include linseed oil. It's a good idea to get rid of some of this before mixing. You can do that by squeezing the paint onto a tissue. The tissue will absorb the linseed oil so that the paint gives a better result when mixed with wax.

The temperature is important when working with hot wax and if you want to try this medium it's a good idea to have a pot which actually keeps the temperature constant at about 200 degrees. If you have it any hotter, it will smoke and that's not a good idea in a studio. At the suggested temperature, it will help the flow of the wax and paint mix on the paintbrush and allow you much time to work with your brush.

Ventilating the studio when working with wax

Remember that heating of wax can cause an odor which is not that healthy to breathe in. It's always better to work in a studio which is well aired. If you can open windows, do so, as this will allow any obnoxious odors to drift away from the studio and allow fresh air in.

Brushes to use for this method of painting

If you decide to experiment with oil and wax, then always use boar hair brushes because they are tough enough to withstand the heat and also help to give you control of your brush strokes. As a beginner, don't expect to get expert overnight with using the mixture of wax and oils, though you may want to try sticks which are already mixed which you can buy at an art shop because these will give you a first taste of what this medium does when used.

Try glazing and cold waxing

If you have done your under-drawing and want to create more light in your image, try using a mixture of linseed oil and galkyp. This is then applied to your palette and the color that you wish to add to your painting is mixed with it. Zinc white is good to add a little lightness into your picture. This is great for applying to a dried painting base because what it does is make the colors translucent and gives the painting a real richness that you can't get simply from using oil paints.

One of the uses that you can put this to is helping to bring out your skin tones and make them look more realistic.

Cold wax medium can be bought at an art shop and is wonderful for enhancing your oil painting techniques. The cold wax is actually in a solid format but liquid enough to mix with colors on your palette and you can use as little or as much as you want, but do bear in mind that too much wax may actually cause peeling at a later stage which would be undesirable. I tend to use more color than wax and find that it just adds a little more texture to the paint than a simple application of paint would give the painting. With the wax you are able to create real texture and that's valuable in a painting but do remember that your actual finish is likely to be matt. If you want to avoid this, add a little linseed oil as this helps your finish to have more of a sheen consistent with the rest of the painting.

One of the ways that artists get around the cracking effect which may happen if too much wax is used is to change the actual material of the painting from using canvas to using something more solid like wood.

This is a great method to experiment with and is particularly good for portraits, miniatures and for scenery and floral designs because of the translucent quality it gives the whole picture. You will have fun with it too because you can add a certain amount of texture and can apply it either with your brushes or with the edge of your palette knife, smoothing it in to the areas where you want the wax to weave its magic.

Chapter 10 – The Great Artists to Emulate

One style that I particularly like is that of Van Gogh because of the textures that are created within his images. You only have to look at the street café image that he created to see what I mean.

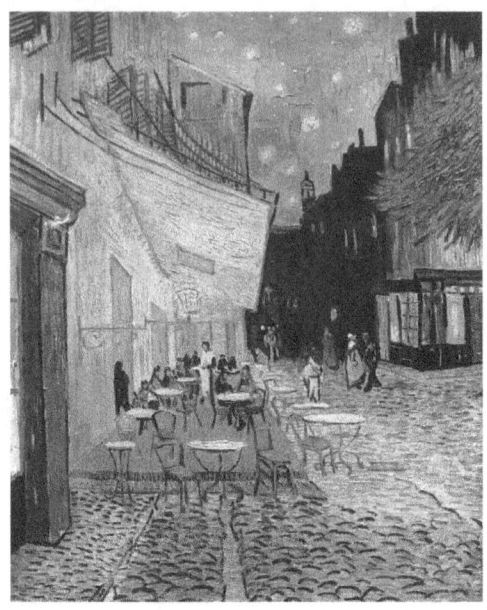

Painted in 1888 the picture shows a street café at night and what is interesting is that he has used texture to give you a real feel of the atmosphere of the place. The cobblestones look real, the sky is studded with stars and the building itself seems to have a texture that is original. Now look to the right of the image and you will see that the tree has wonderful texture as well and layering creates all this.

After Van Gogh painted the street café, he wrote a very famous letter to his sister explaining all about the way that he viewed the colors of the street and had to paint them the way that he saw them, rather than using dull light and more realistic colors. His enthusiasm showed in that letter and he continued with his works until his death in 1890, just two years after the painting of this image. A painting that followed the street café and which used the same style to depict a landscape was the Country Road in Provence which was painted in the year of his death and which uses vibrant color a little more stark than the café painting, but in the very same style that people know and love today.

Many new artists aspire to creating the same layered effects and do so quite adequately, so don't think that you can't attempt this style and create something unique. Every brushstroke and every system of painting is of course very individual and it may be your painting that people are talking about years from now.

The history of oil painting

Going back in history, you may be surprised to know that the first people to use oil painting were Buddhist painters who discovered the medium as far back as the 15th century. Oil painting became a classic way of presenting art and because of its popularity as a medium, traveled worldwide during the Middle Ages and has been used ever since. Although other forms of artwork have also recently become popular, oil painting is the kind of art that one associates with the greatest of paintings.

No greater example can be shown than the Mona Lisa, by Leonardo da Vinci, painted between 1503 and 1506, which still shows today the skill of the artist to make the model so realistic that people believe her eyes follow you as you move from one side of the painting to another. The detail was extraordinary. The pigments used in old masters would oftentimes be those which didn't come in bought tubes but which were mixed by the artist himself. That's why buying and trying pigments really will add value to the work that you do, because the variety of colors that these provide is extraordinary.

Different medium was used as a backdrop to many famous oil paintings and in particular the self-portrait of Rembrandt, which was painted in 1630 was painted on copper instead of canvas and has held up to the test of time. Renaissance painters experimented with different types of medium as well and were the first users of wooden background panels for their oil paints. These were very successful and gave a stable surface to the paintings.

Looking at the quality of paintings such as La Donna Valeta, which was produced by Raphael in 1516, one cannot help but be amazed by the amount of rich texture that was produced by the artist and still looks every bit as flowing today as it did then.

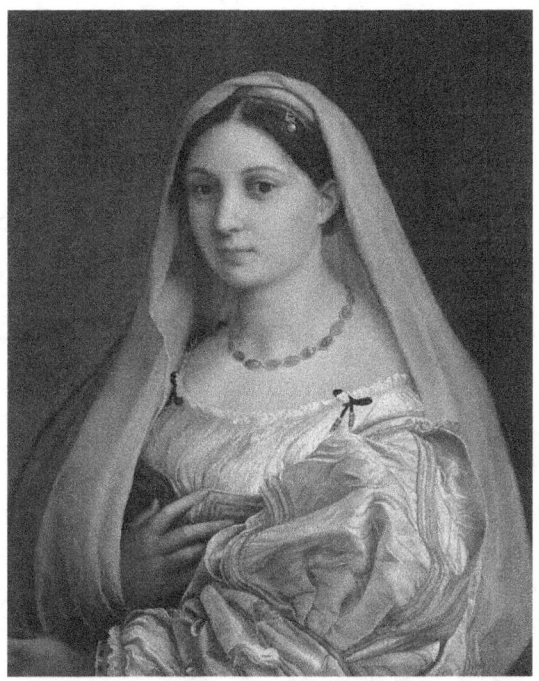

The skin tones are perfect and the three dimensional effect superb. Look at the way the fabric folds and the detail in the facial features of this classic pose. It's worth noting that you can produce this translucence today much more easily than it was produced in those days because there are far more materials available for the artist to experiment with which are already prepared.

As a new artist, looking at what has been produced inspires you because you choose your style according to your own preferences, but these examples show what can be done with oils to produce a wonderful painting and learning from the masters is one of the best ways to begin your experience.

Johann Vermeer produced this astounding image as early as in 1658-1660 but what is so amazing about this picture is the depth of the colors used. Remember, the paints would have been mixed from natural pigments and the depth of the blue in this image is such that it has lasted for centuries, still looking every bit as dazzling today as it did then.

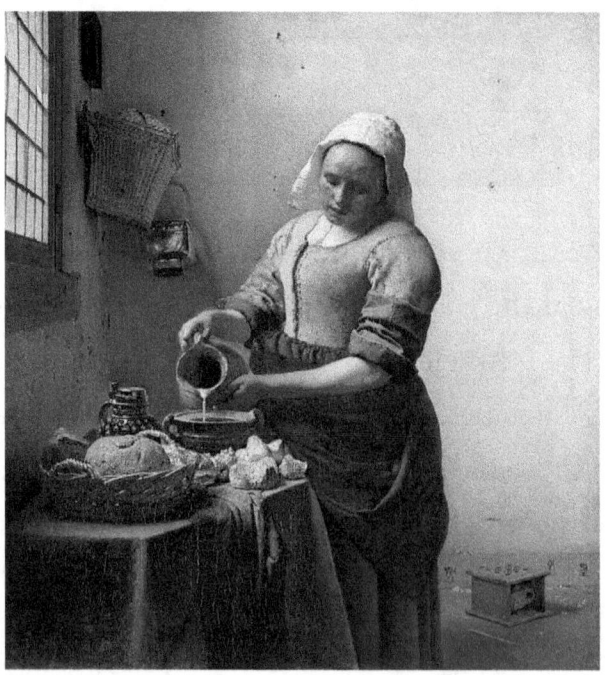

Paintings become an historical record of the times of the painter. Thus, they are very important from an historical point of view and thus painted in oils, the pictures retain their quality and give us a glimpse into the past with great accuracy. The paintings of the masters also give us ideas on how to use color, composition and subject matter that remain of interest and the longevity of a painting will depend upon its appeal to the viewer.

Judith Ann Miller

Chapter 11 – Finding out More about Pigments

In the last chapter, we told you about the pigments that were used for historical artwork and today an artist has a chance to reproduce that quality because pigments are still available. At the very beginning of your painting experience, it's likely that you will stick to tubes of paint, but there will come a time when you will want to take a step further and learn about producing your own colors using pigments.

Types of pigments

Oil Sticks

In the olden days, the only kinds of pigments that were used were derived from plants. In this day and age, there are different types that can be bought in art shops, which have been developed for the use of the modern painter. For example, oil sticks made with 100 percent pigments give wonderful color value, ready to use for the artist of today. These are an introduction to the artist and are great value from several perspectives. One is that they are ready to use and the other is that the pigments have been chosen to give the best color rendition. These come in all of the natural shades such as yellow ochre, burnt sienna, red ochre, mars violet, mars black and titanium white and of course many others.

When you open an oil stick you may find it a little strange to use although the way that this is applied is by using it like a child would use a crayon. You will need some mineral spirits and you also need a good quality brush. Apply the paint in the area of your canvas where you want the color to appear. The paint is then worked with your brush dipped in a little mineral spirits or thinners and this gives you better control over what the color is doing on the canvas and the thickness of it. Remember that oil sticks are made with wax and once you open the stick and wipe off the wax seal, you have paint ready to use with pigments that are already mixed for you. Oil sticks can be used over dried oils as well so that makes them ideal for detailing. They will dry in a couple of hours and are very convenient to carry around, rather than having to work with tubes and a palette.

Dry Pigments

Mixing Egg Tempera

If you ever wondered what makes the oil paint that you buy in tubes, it's made from mixing pigments with oil such as linseed oil, but that isn't the only way that colors were mixed. In olden times, egg tempera was used and essentially this is a mixture of dry pigments and egg white. To do this kind of mix, the pigment is diluted in water until it actually resembles paint.

However, you need to understand that at this stage, it isn't paint and if you were to use it, it's likely that when it dries, the pigment would merely wipe off your canvas surface with your hand. Using egg yolk as a binder helps it to stick together and to stay in the form of oil paint. If you watch an artist mixing paint in this way, chances are that you will see them using a glass tool to press onto the mixture to get rid of any powder that may remain in the mixture. Mix in a small amount of yolk and your paint is ready to use. In this case, it's not strictly oil paint as it is water based. It is actually linseed or other oils that make pigments into oil paint.

Mixing pigments with linseed oil

This is a messy business and you need to make sure that the surface upon which you are working gives sufficient protection to areas around the mixing. If not, you may find that spillage is a possibility. If you are going to be mixing your oil paints on a regular basis, it is worthwhile investing in the following tools that will help you:

- A mixing board
- A glass muller
- Linseed oil
- Powder pigments
- A respirator

The reason why a respirator is so important is that some pigments are toxic and if you breathe them in, they really won't be very good for your health. Thus, this part of the equipment is necessary.

If you have a shop with tubes available in which to place your paints, these are a great way to store paint between uses and you can mix larger batches of color all at the same time labeling your tube with the color mix that is contained in it. That way, uniformity is assured. It's also a good idea to have throwaway gloves and to make sure that your clothing is protected during the mixing process. You may have seen traditional artists wearing smocks and they have good cause. Pigments can cause stains.

One of the reasons that safety precautions need to be adhered to is that many pigments are lead based and this is dangerous, so be sure to protect yourself from inhalation, from getting pigments in the eyes and keep your hands and clothing protected.

Linseed oil is the choice of most artists because it gives a fair amount of time for you to work the paint before it dries. Other oils are more liquid and tend to be difficult to work with, and as paints bought in tubes use linseed, these seems to be the natural choice for the artist mixing their own paints. Purists will use other oils for their mix but the disadvantage of these is that they dry too slowly and even if you were to add a dryer to the mix, what happens is that you risk cracking of the surface and that's not at all attractive. Linseed is therefore the safest choice and although it yellows a little with time, this adds to the attraction of the painting.

Remember that cadmium and all the metal based pigments are the dangerous ones to breathe in as these can give you lead poisoning. Thus handling these with care and using the correct safety gear really do make sense.

On your mixing board, pour out enough of the pigment powder and built it up like a hill with a hole in the center. Pour the linseed oil into the hole and gradually work in the pigment with the palette knife. People are usually a little nervous when they first mix their own colors, but you need the consistency to be creamy so that it resembles paint.

At this stage you start to use the muller. What this does is press the paint and if you move it in a figure of eight over the paint, this makes sure that all of the pigment is mixed in and that there are no lumpy areas. If you add too much oil, the paint will have a shine to it and will not stand up in peaks. In this case, add more pigment. The best kind of mixing board is made of glass because this doesn't absorb the paint as you are making it. Remember if you mix your white paint thick, you can always thin it when you use it and this uses less oil and will thus yellow less.

Natural Dye Pigments

These are used in much the same way as powder pigments and again, it's wise to use a respirator and protect your eyes. These give natural colors and some purists prefer to use the natural dye pigments rather than those that are manufactured. The system to blending these with the oil is exactly the same as shown above.

Chapter 12 – Effects You Can Create With Oil Paints

There are many ways to apply oil paints to your canvas and the different effects are wonderful. You need to experiment with these different ways to see what effect they give. We have already talked about using wax but it's the application that we will cover in this chapter.

Applying oil paints straight from tubes

When you are working with oil paints, you will find that they have a certain thickness. You can apply oils directly from the tubes and take advantage of this thickness to build up layers but this thickness and the mixing of wax into the color is usually done after the under-drawing is finished. Otherwise, the textures and the effects that are created may be lost. Thus, feel free to use paint directly from the tubes and by mixing it on your palette but if these were to be colors that simply form the first layers of the painting, you would be wise to thin them a little and apply them with a fairly large brush. You can turn your brush at different angles much like calligraphers turn the nib of their pen, because this gives you more control over the amount of paint, which is placed, on the canvas.

Adding Wax to Oil Paints

As discussed before, this is a very good way to build up texture and opacity. There are several ways that you can apply the paint once it is mixed. If it is liquid enough, you can use a paintbrush and paint areas that you want to have a little more color or brightness. If you were drawing a window, adding the wax and oil paint mix would help to diffuse the light and make it much more realistic looking.

You can also apply this kind of mixture to landscapes to highlight different areas or to make the hills in the distance stand out from the sky beyond it. This is detail work and is usually done after the under-drawing and as part of the finishing of the painting. The color mixed with the wax will give you a great depth of color once it is applied but be aware that you may need to use a glaze since these areas may look a little flat. You can also mix in a little linseed oil to get the shine on the paint or at least to make it look like it is a satin finish as opposed to a matt finish.

Using Boar Brushes

Boar brushes are a lot harder than other brushes. The hairs are pretty stiff and this makes the brush perfect for applying texture. Dab the brush into the paint and then dab onto the image and you get a series of colors and shapes that give a painting a lot more detail. For example, leaves on trees, shrubs next to a lake, or even adding to skin texture with the use of a boar brush can help the color build up and also draw the viewer into the three dimensional elements of the picture. This doesn't have to be a finished look since after you have applied the paint and while it is still a little damp, you can calm down areas where too much texture was added by using a wax mixture.

Using a Palette Knife

This is a superb way to make your paint lift from the canvas. It's also a way to spread paint easily. Once you learn the subtleties of using the palette knife you will also learn that it can give very sharp detail when you apply the paint with the tip of the palette knife to give a raised effect. This is particularly relevant to facial features such as the lower lip or areas such as the nostrils and the palette knife is something you need to practice with because all kinds of effects can be achieved using it. Your paint should be fairly thick when you use a palette knife and you can even use this with a wax and oil paint mix because this consistency is perfect for palette knife application.

Using Detail Brushes

When your picture is nearing completion, you may want to add fine detail to it. This is best achieved with detail brushes that are smaller than other brushes and allow you to create fine lines. Practice with detailing because it's an important part of oil painting. The lines of a fence in the garden or the lines of white down the side of a tree, which give the trunk more depth and roundness, are all important finishing touches. In the image earlier in the book where we showed you the detail of an eye, this would have been achieved using detail brushes and building up layers, which made the eventual eye look almost transparent and watery.

Detail brushes in different sizes are essential as these can give you the exact size of line that you want to create. Thus, if you find your detailing isn't fine enough, switch to a smaller brush. You can always repaint over the area with the base colors and start again, although you will get accustomed to choosing the right size with time and experience.

Judith Ann Miller

Chapter 13 – Keeping Your Painting Equipment Clean

One of the elements that you must have in the studio is thinner. These are used to help clean your brushes, but the cleaning does not end there. It does form an important part of the cleaning process, though other cleaning elements are discussed as well in this chapter.

Cleaning Brushes

Remember that oil paints only have a set time before they dry. If you let the paint dry into the stock of the brush, you will ruin your brushes. You may have noticed that many artists have jam jars in their studios where they place brushes between uses and these will have solvents in them, so that the colored paint seeps out of the brush. This isn't sufficient cleaning and you will need to take all of your brushes and put them into clean thinners at the end of each session, being sure to work into the stock of the brush until there is no more paint left. The clean brush can be shaken outside to remove any excess liquid after being washed in soapy water once all the paint is removed by the thinners.

The soapy water helps to keep the brushes supple, but must be rinsed out thoroughly. Never push your brush down into the sink while cleaning it because you can destroy the integrity of the brush. Instead, be very gentle and respect your brushes, cleaning the metal part above the bristles, the stock of the brush where the bristles go into the metal and the tips of the brush. If you have accidentally left a brush too long, you may be lucky and may be able to get the paint off by soaking it in thinners but be careful that the bristles are always straight. It's very easy to forget that you have brushes soaked and if the head of the brush bends, it can be ruined.

Cleaning Palette Knives

Since these are generally made of stainless steel, it's wise to have cloths in the studio so that they can be wiped clean while the paint is still damp. If you do need a little thinner to get any awkward bits of paint off, this is quite acceptable, though it's important to keep palette knives clean because if they are left to have a build-up of paint, the edge that you depend upon may soften and spoil the use of the knife. Thus keeping it clean should be part of your painting routine.

Cleaning Your Palette

There are not many artists that have clean palettes. This is because it's the main mixing area for the paints and as you work and the thinner layers dry, the palette becomes clogged up with paint. However, if you use a paint scraper when you have finished with a particular color and keep the surface of the palette flat, you can control it to a certain degree. Wiping off the palette is another option that is open to you, although it's messy and you will need to finish off the clean with thinners. As long as the surface is flat, that's really all that matters when you go to do your next mix.

Cleaning Your Muller

The muller is made of glass and is therefore very easy to clean if you do this straight away. The handle of a muller has a flat area that you push down on when you are mixing your paints. Clean the whole muller including this top part because clean glass produces wonderfully soft and creamy paints and it would be a real shame to let any paint gather on the surface of the glass. If you should forget to clean it straight away, you may need to use thinners, but try to avoid too much abrasion since you may cause pitting in the glass and this is never a very good idea.

Cleaning Your Mixing Boards

Make it a habit to clean these as soon as you have mixed your pigments with linseed oil. When you have placed the paint into its tube, clean the board. This is vital to future mixes since having the remains of a mix may spoil the quality of the next mix.

Studio Cleanliness in General

Get into good habits from the start because having a messy studio can really play havoc with tools and materials and it's worthwhile remembering that the results of your work depend upon being produced with tools that are well looked after. Clean the easel occasionally to ensure that it is all functional and if the adjustment is getting stiff, then you may need to add a little wax to keep the pegs, which allow you to adjust the easel easy to move when needed.

Chapter 14 – 7 Quick Tips to Improve at Oil Painting

1. **Paint, Paint, Paint. Then Paint Some More.**

    The best way to improve at painting is to keep painting. When you are starting out, it is good to focus on making several short-term works. This way you can get quick feedback in between your works so you can improve on the next one. The more you paint and the more of your works are critiqued, by you or others, the more information you have to improve.

    If you want to try a new technique don't be afraid of it. Remember that you will learn from your own mistakes and in order to do that, you need to give yourself the experience to actually make mistakes sometimes as these are the best lessons that you can get. Thus, keep painting and trying new techniques because when you find one that really suits your style, you will be thrilled, just like Van Gogh was when he wrote to his sister about the street café painting and what he had discovered about his representation of light. At the time the guy painted the picture, he would certainly not have known the historical impact that painting would have and it was by trial and error that he learned.

2. **Go to Art Class**

It pays to take a class since it gives you the benefit of an expert both teaching you and evaluating you. It also ensures that you paint on schedule. Aim for classes that teach fundamentals and not specific styles of the instructors. It is much better to get a handle on the basics so you can develop a style of your own.

If you find that you don't see eye to eye with a teacher, try another. It may be that they are stuck in their ways. You can also get classes online and it's worthwhile looking at your local library for details of classes in your area as well as finding out what books can help you hand in hand with classes.

3. **Gather Information**

Read up on painting. There is a wide selection of books, videos, audios and articles on oil painting. The more information you can gather, the more you can channel into developing your skills. With the boom of information on the Internet, you can now even take classes online. One thing which is very worthwhile is watching YouTube videos because the instruction is split into different sections. Supposing for example you want to learn to mix your pigments in a different way or experiment with different colors and textures. Artists who have achieved great results are quick to share information on places such as YouTube and an afternoon of learning from watching fellow artists at work will really help your style and the techniques that you use.

4. **Lots of Preparation**

Some of the best works are the best because of extensive preparation. Make sure you have the proper materials. Research on what you have to. Make sketches or under-drawings before you paint. Arrange the structure of your work before you put it to the canvas. Even getting in the proper state of mind before you work can do wonders for you. Use the technology around you to help you with your compositions. IPad is ideal because you can take a picture of the scene and then take from different angles and have an instant idea of which angle gives you the better composition.

If you have all the right tools and are prepared for your first painting, you will also have a good idea of the kind of color wheel you will need to use to produce the colors that you are aiming at. Play around with oil sticks as these are very useful to get an idea of what oils can do. Applied directly onto the paper, you can draw out your shapes with them but they do much more than that.

Dilute what is on the canvas by using thinners and you can almost create the same kind of opacity that one would expect to get from water-colors. Have everything you need for your first session in the studio ready before you start, pour yourself a cup of coffee and settle down to a session of painting. You need to organize your time if you want to be productive and as with most arts, each time you do, you need to incorporate new things, so that your portfolio of images is diverse enough for you to recognize your strengths and weaknesses.

5. **Keep the Good and Drop the Bad**

   Do not be afraid to scrap a part of your painting or most of it if you know that it is bad. You will make mistakes while you paint and you might realize this only after you spent much time and effort on them. But remember that taking a long time to paint is nothing compared to leaving a bad portion of your work ruin the rest of it. Remember that even the great artists of history were known to paint over large portions of their own work if they felt unsatisfied with it.

The main thing to remember is to get your proportions right on your under-drawing. This helps you to be more accurate with your actual finishing and makes the picture look much better. The areas that people often have to overpaint are features like bad backgrounds, eye detail, placement of facial features, heads not in proportion with bodies, etc. Don't worry about having to redo it because you are learning all the time that you are doing this.

6. **Paint the Real Stuff**

Some of the best art is already around you. Painting from real life is a better way to learn how to paint than using photographs or stock pictures since you can actually see how the subject interacts with its environment. It is this interaction that you want to capture and bring to life on the canvas. This does not mean painting from photographs is inferior, but if you want to learn how to paint well, learn from real life.

You can use real life models and use the iPad to help you in the proportions and the layout of your composition, but don't rely totally upon technology to do it for you. That interaction between an artist and his subject is very important. Robert Lenkiewicz was an artist who died in recent years, but whose work really reflected the relationship between himself and the subjects he painted. Many of his works examine his relationship with himself and are self-portraits. The relationship between you and the model should shine through in the image that you produce, just like it does in the work of Lenkiewicz.

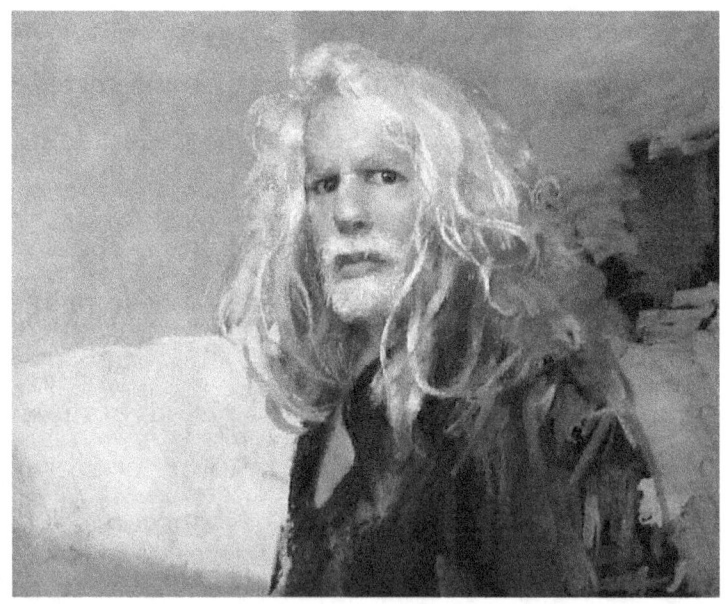

7. Stare at Some Art

The best way to learn painting is to learn from the masters. You can do this by taking a look at how the great oil painters painted. When you study artwork, make sure to look for originals and not reproductions. The original art will show you how the masters used strokes and solved problems in their work that you will most likely encounter. Imagine you were painting their work, and then ask: How did they portray shadows? How did they paint skin? How do they show details on a flower? All these and more can be ascertained just by looking closely at their work.

Judith Ann Miller

Conclusion

Thank you again for purchasing this book!

I hope this book was able to help you get a head start in your career as an oil painter. Hopefully with the simple principles and techniques you learned here, you can graduate into more advanced painting techniques and even develop new techniques of your own. Strive to make these techniques your own and develop your own style.

The book has given you a lot of information about oil painting, the use of pigments, the addition of wax and other medium to help you to produce wonderful pictures. You will be able to use this as a guide as you walk through the experience of becoming an oil painter. Even if your canvas is small and your attempt relatively humble, remember that famous artists also had humble beginnings and that we now recognize the work that was put into classic masterpieces that have gone on to become part of the world in which we live. Everyone knows and recognizes many of these paintings and some of these have been featured in this book because of their style merit which may help you to develop your own style and follow in the footsteps of the great artists of the past.

If you are keen to start your experience, do take the advice of the book and also seek classes as these will reinforce the principles which are laid out within the pages of this book. Look also for supplementary information in the form of videos because often watching practical application can teach you an awful lot. People learn from a very early age from using imitation and that's where videos will help you because they show you an example of a certain element of oil painting and you can see the practicality of why people do things in set ways.

Many artists all over the world are showing their work on websites specifically designed to give new artists a gallery and yours may one day be among those images. It isn't a great stretch of the imagination to have ambition in that direction since the Internet offers a worldwide marketplace for artists and also plenty of websites where critiques can help you with your techniques. It is hoped that this book will help you move toward becoming a very enthusiastic artist and once who is not afraid of experimentation and producing images which really do you justice. You never know, you may be the next Vincent Van Gogh!

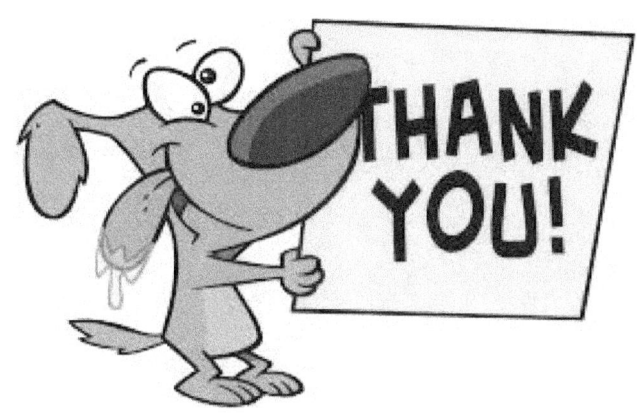

Bonus Video: Oil Painting Tips, Tricks, Techniques. Things the other videos don't tell you. Tutorial

Enjoy this Bonus video on oil painting techniques and tricks.

Free Video: https://www.youtube.com/watch?v=roIAXvL04PA

Judith Ann Miller

Check Out My Other Books

- http://www.amazon.com/Acrylic-Painting-Techniques-Landscape-Everything-ebook/dp/B00Q3SRQJG/ref=sr_1_5?s=digital-text&ie=UTF8&qid=1421113485&sr=1-5&keywords=painting

- http://www.amazon.com/Painting-Box-Acrylic-Guide-Beginners-ebook/dp/B00UTNRGNW/ref=sr_1_6?s=digital-text&ie=UTF8&qid=1441313269&sr=1-6&keywords=painting&pebp=1441313273173&perid=1S3K51G50BMZE8BE21QQ

- http://www.amazon.com/Painting-Techniques-Beginners-Watercolor-Acrylic-ebook/dp/B00WUJF72O/ref=sr_1_1?s=digital-text&ie=UTF8&qid=1441314244&sr=1-1&keywords=painting&pebp=1441314246282&perid=1MRM4QPX5BVXXQCRA9W4

Judith Ann Miller

www.ingramcontent.com/pod-product-compliance
Lightning Source LLC
Chambersburg PA
CBHW070820180526
45168CB00002B/697